# The Grand Retablo

Rev. William Krekelberg

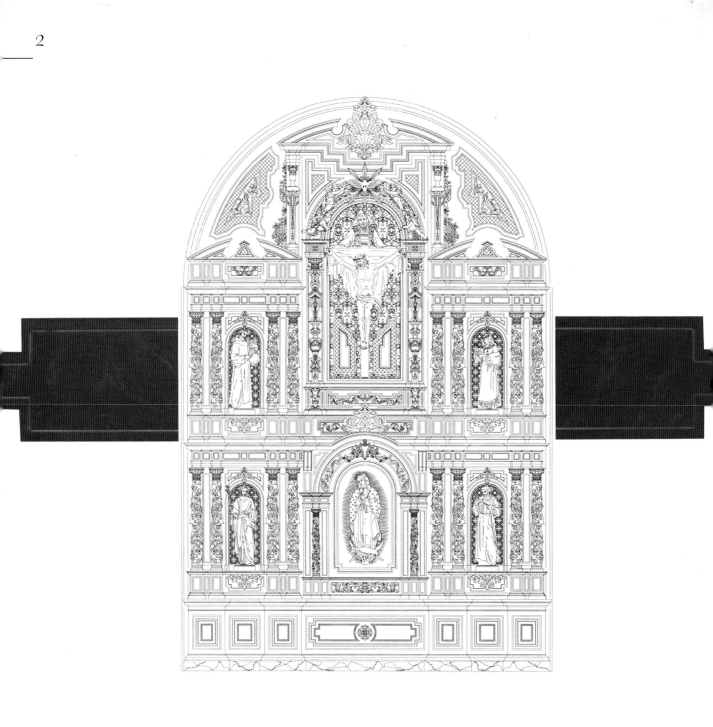

# TABLE OF Contents

Pope Benedict XVI

## William Joseph Levada

*Archbishop Emeritus of San Francisco*
*Prefect of the Congregation for the Doctrine of the Faith*

Created a Cardinal
of the Holy Roman Church
in the Consistory of March 24, 2006

In the first year of the pontificate
of

# BENEDICT XVI

*"Quam bonum et quam iucundum*
*habitare fratres in unum"*

Psalm 133

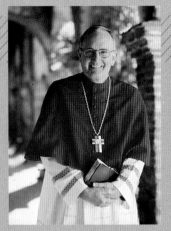

# Diocese of Orange

July 21, 2007

Dear Brothers and Sisters in Christ,

Congratulations to all of you on the installation of the magnificent Retablo!

As the Constitution on the Sacred Liturgy notes, "These (sacred) arts by their very nature are oriented toward the infinite beauty of God, which they attempt to portray by the work of human hands. They are dedicated to advancing God's praise and glory to the degree that they center on the single aim of turning the human spirit devoutly toward God." (Constitution on the Sacred Liturgy, Ch. VII.122). The Mission Retablo not only inspires such awe but will serve to educate by the symbolism that is portrayed in the design and construction of this outstanding work of art.

The Mission complex has long attracted thousands of visitors each year. The addition of the Retablo will add to that powerful pilgrim experience that has captured our imaginations and aided in the understanding of our early California history.

We are blessed to have this extraordinary addition to our Church in Orange.

In Christ Our Savior,
Most Reverend Tod D. Brown, D.D.
Bishop of the Diocese of Orange

†Tod D Brown

# Mission Basilica San Juan Capistrano
## *A National Shrine*

$\mathcal{D}$ear Friends,

It is with great joy that the faith community of Mission San Juan Capistrano mark the long anticipated completion of the interior of the Basilica Church with the installation of the magnificent Grand Retablo together with the renovation of other significant areas within the sanctuary. In his recent Apostolic Exhortation entitled, Sacramentum Caritatis, our Holy Father, Pope Benedict XVI, states:

*The profound connection between beauty and the liturgy should make us attentive to every work of art placed at the service of the celebration. Certainly an important element of sacred art is church architecture, which should highlight the unity of the furnishings of the sanctuary, such as the altar, the crucifix, the tabernacle, the ambo and the celebrant's chair.*

*Here it is important to remember that the purpose of sacred architecture is to offer the Church a fitting space for the celebration of the mysteries of faith, especially the Eucharist. The very nature of a Christian church is defined by the liturgy, which is an assembly of the faithful (ecclesia) who are the living stones of the Church (cf. 1 Pet 2:5).*

For over 230 years, Mission San Juan Capistrano has been a place of both pilgrimage and peace. May the renewed beauty of our Basilica Church now enhanced by our magnificent Grand Retablo continue to be an inspiration for all who journey in faith to this place whose ground has been hallowed by the sons of St. Francis. May the motto of Blessed Junipero Serra be a touchstone of hope for all who visit this "Jewel" of the California Missions, "Always forward!"

In the Lord, Very Reverend
Arthur A. Holquin
Rector/Pastor

# MISSION BASILICA
# San Juan Capistrano

## HISTORICAL OVERVIEW

In 1769, Spanish soldiers and missionaries arrived in Alta California to claim the territory for the King (Carlos III) and the King of Kings (Jesus Christ). In 1776, Blessed Fray Junipero Serra founded California's seventh mission, San Juan Capistrano.

✤ Sacred Garden

San Juan Capistrano ✤

Of the twenty-one missions eventually established, San Juan Capistrano became one of its most productive, both spiritually and materially. At its height, it boasted of over a thousand Christian Indian converts. It also recorded huge agricultural harvests and many thousands of livestock. Besides teaching religion, it taught fundamental methods of carpentry, building, blacksmithing, cloth weaving, farming, irrigation, and ranching.

The Mission was so successful that authorities allowed it to build what was then the grandest and most ambitious church in California. Work began on the Great Stone Church in 1797 and finished in 1806. The California Governor, Jose Joaquin de Arrillaga, and Fray Estevan Tapis, President of the Missions, along with other dignitaries and the proud Indian builders, celebrated the event in a fiesta that lasted several days.

Tragically, the Great Stone Church collapsed in a major earthquake that struck California in 1812. Its majestic ruins still stand in silent testimony to the noble efforts of its builders and those who lost their lives in its destruction.

In 1822, Mexico achieved its independence from Spain. In 1833, the California Missions were secularized and its vast Indian estates were divided into land grants.

These became the great ranchos of the Californios. In 1845, Governor Pio Pico auctioned Mission San Juan Capistrano into private hands. The following year, the United States and Mexico were at war with each other. In 1848, California became a U. S. possession. And in 1850, California became the 31st State of the United States. Following much litigation, Mission San Juan Capistrano (its buildings and immediate surrounding property) was restored to the Catholic Church in 1865 by a patent of title signed by President Abraham Lincoln. During the 1890s, serious efforts were made to preserve this historic site. This endeavor continues to the present day.

## THE BUILDING

Although there were efforts to repair and rebuild the Great Stone Church, limited resources and changing demographics prevented it. However in modern times, population growth in the area made a new church both possible and necessary.

Rather than disturb the ancient ruins and rebuild on the original site, parishioners decided to preserve them and build a new church in its image and

likeness at its present location directly behind the Old Mission. This new church carefully followed the details of the original, but was proportionately larger to accommodate the increased population. Modern methods and materials were employed to guard against the threat of future earthquakes and provide greater safety for its occupants. Groundbreaking for this new parish church took place on January 31, 1982. The church opened for use in 1985 and was solemnly dedicated by Cardinal Timothy Manning of February 8, 1987.

## THE BASILICA

MISSION BASILICA
SAN JUAN CAPISTRANO

Major basilicas are the principal papal churches associated with early Christian Rome. The main ones are St. John Lateran, St. Peter's at the Vatican, St. Paul's Outside the Walls, and St. Mary Major. These have been important pilgrimage centers down through the years.

At the millennium, on February 14th in the Jubilee and Holy Year of 2000, His Holiness Pope John Paul II honored the Mission Church of San Juan Capistrano with the title of a Minor Basilica. A Minor Basilica is so honored because of its special historic, cultural, and devotional importance. It is required that such a church be an example as an active faith community with very high standards in the celebration of its liturgies. Because of its papal recognition, it maintains a special relationship with the Holy See and is expected to offer prayers for the Holy Father, especially on feast days related to the papacy and days related to the reigning pope, such as the anniversary of his pontificate.

# BASILICA SYMBOLS

## PAPEL CREST

A church honored as a basilica becomes a special gathering place, a pilgrimage center, for the larger faith community and bears a special bond with the Holy See from which it received its title. The basilica symbols illustrate both this charge and this relationship.

On the outside of the Mission Basilica, over the principal entrances, the official coat of arms of the reigning pontiff, Pope Benedict XVI, announces in symbol that pilgrims are entering a special place both honored by and dedicated to the Holy Father.

## TINTINABELLUM
### Basilica Bell

On the right side of the sanctuary is a silver bell characteristic of a basilica. It is also a symbol of papacy and pilgrimage. In olden times, a silver bell preceded the Holy Father's journeys and alerted people to his approach so that they might come and pay their respects and receive his blessing. San Juan Capistrano's basilica bell is a crown bell. (Bells given to the California Missions with a crown on top were royal bells donated by the King.) The bell is also decorated with the Mission's characteristic swallows The stones on the frame's four corners are malachite. The decoration at the top of the pole and the bottom of the frame is designed to represent the four evangelists: Matthew, Mark, Luke, and John. This bell, manufactured in Holland by Stadelmaier of Nijmegan, is carried in procession at solemn liturgies.

### *OMBRELLINO*
### *Basilica Umbrella*

Inside the sanctuary, near the ambo (pulpit), is a basilica ombrellino. It is reminiscent of the days long past when a processional umbrella protected the Holy Father from the elements on his travels. The red and gold colors, borrowed from the tradition of the Roman Senate, testified to his spiritual authority. Along its edges, the Mission Basilica's ombrellino is decorated with a variety of relevant coats of arms. This ombrellino , manufactured by Stadelmaier, is also carried in procession at solemn liturgies.

Basilica Date of Designation

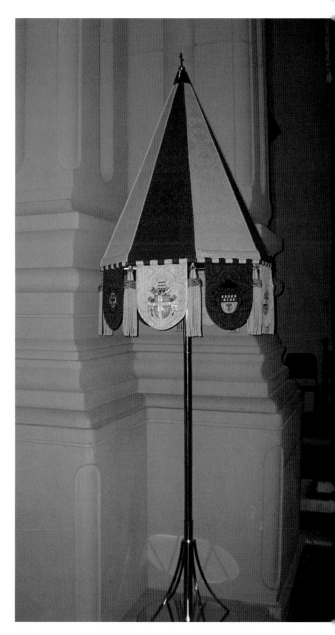

Pope John Paul II

Diocese of Orange

Bishop Tod D. Brown

Basilica San Juan
Capistrano

Franciscan Order

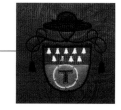

San Juan
Capistrano

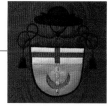

Blessed
Junipero Serra

## *A NATIONAL SHRINE*

On the Feast of Saint Joseph, March 19, 2003, the U. S. National Conference of Catholic Bishops designated Mission San Juan Capistrano as a National Shrine. This high honor was in recognition of the Mission's "effective service to the spiritual, liturgical, and devotional life of pilgrims" from across the United States and the international community. As a National Shrine, Mission Basilica San Juan Capistrano is an officially sanctioned and recommended place of pilgrimage. It is dedicated to inspiring and fostering the deeper spiritual renewal sought by religious pilgrims.

# THE GRAND
## *Retablo*

Retablo is a Spanish word and literally means behind the table or altar. It could be as simple as a shelf or ledge that hold the altar cross, candles, and, perhaps, flowers. It could also be an elaborate framework, or altarpiece, such as the Grand Retablo of this Mission Basilica. Or, it can be something in between with appropriate liturgical art such as a background for a mosaic, painting, or other decorative items relating to the altar and the place.

A retablo – sometimes called a rererdos –is the background that enhances the altar which is the liturgical focal point of the sanctuary. The retablo is not meant to be distinct from the altar; rather, it is its extension and adornment. Indeed, sometimes a retablo is simply called an altar. This was especially true when, in the past, the altar table was built into it and the Mass was celebrated with the priest facing the retablo and his back to the congregation.

## ⤲ THE PERSPECTIVE

*Our prayer of thanksgiving adds nothing to your greatness, but make us grow in your grace.*
*(Preface 40)*

Certainly, we do not impress God by even our best artistic creations. Our buildings, statues, paintings, and our ornate sacred vessels do not wow God who made the wonders and beauty of creation. Why do we do them then? Is it vanity, or folly, or both? One could question whether or not it might be better to put our efforts to charitable causes: Give it to the poor.

### *ALL FOR THE GLORY OF GOD*

While charity is our essential Christian virtue and mission, it does not exclude our natural desire to express our best in a way that may inspire others to a sense of the presence of God in their lives.

People are endowed with various talents and skills. It is good when a person wants to use those gifts in a special way to glorify God. A skilled craftsman would like his best work to be offered to God. Skilled architects, engineers, builders, and artists naturally express gratitude for their abilities by doing the best they can in God's service. It is not a matter of impressing God. It is a matter of doing their personal best to inspire God's people.

*The fine arts are deservedly ranked among the noblest activities of human genius and this applies especially to religious art and to its highest achievement, sacred art.*
*(Vatican II, Constitution on the Liturgy, 122)*

# BAROQUE

The Grand Retablo is in the baroque style that flourished from the end of the 16th Century to the late 18th. This style is a dramatic departure from a previous emphasis on elegant simplicity in form and function. Baroque artists wanted something new, different, and daring. Traditionalists considered this artistic heresy and for them "baroque" meant anything odd, eccentric, bizarre, and generally in bad taste.

Nevertheless, the style caught on and enjoyed a long run in usage and popularity. Classic lines, theoretical limits, and traditional forms were out. The new, baroque fashion emphasized free imagination and an exuberant liberty. It was a triumph of imagination and vitality, characterized by heavy ornamentation and decoration. Where straight lines could be curved, it was preferred. Where columns could be twisted and spiraled, they were.

Facades were broken into sections. Decorated columns, pillars, broken pediments and cornices were in high fashion. Statues looked like they might "step from their niches" – dynamic and intensely mystical, an impression advanced by the use of polychrome. Empty spaces (Horror Vacui) could not be tolerated. All must be alive. Foliage, roses, vines, and grapes are typical decorations. The baroque thrived on life, movement, and an unrelenting play of light and shadow. Such is the style of the Grand Retablo.

A theological consideration about the baroque retablo is also relevant. During the period of the Reformation, certain theologians argued that the Liturgy of the Eucharist (the Mass) must focus on the communal meal (the Lord's Supper) wherein we enter into a Holy Communion with Jesus and one another. Traditional theologians argued that the Mass is the renewal of Jesus' sacrifice on the cross whereby we are redeemed and saved. In the Counter Reformation, larger, more realistic crucifixes and grander retablos emphasized this traditional theological perspective. The Church's position on this issue was made clear for all to see. The argument was taken up again at the Second Vatican Council. The result and approved view was that these two perspectives, Mass as Sacrifice and Sacred Communal Meal, were not mutually exclusive. They complimented one another and both have their importance in a complete understanding of the Liturgy of the Eucharist.

# ✒THE INSPIRATION

Mission San Juan Capistrano was founded during the period when baroque art was flourishing. Of course, humble mission churches did not have the elegant retablos that could be found in cathedrals and major churches in Spain and its well-established colonies. The missionaries had seen them. And they did their best to provide quality vestments and accoutrements worthy of the Sacred Liturgy, but something as beautiful and elaborate as the Grand Retablo was out of the question.

Inspiration for the basilica retablo is taken from the beautiful "Golden Altar" that adorns the Serra Chapel. That retablo is actually considerably older than the Mission itself. Early in the 1900's, this centuries old retablo was purchased in Spain and intended for a new cathedral in Los Angeles. Eventually, cathedral plans were set aside and the retablo remained stored in packing crates in the old cathedral's basement.

In 1924, Archbishop John J. Cantwell offered this hand-carved masterpiece to Father St. John O'Sullivan, pastor of the Mission, who was then restoring its Serra Chapel. Everyone then, and now, who visits this historic chapel recognizes what an appropriate and beautiful addition this retablo made to the over all experience of this sacred space.

Naturally, when the new parish church of San Juan Capistrano opened in 1985, it was hoped that in the future some such grand altarpiece might adorn its sanctuary. It would be a fine work of art that would inspire people, drawing them closer to God through the experience of its beauty. Nevertheless, it was a question of time and the wherewithal. In the intervening years, there were other pressing needs demanding attention.

Following the Millennium and Holy Year, 2000, the concept and possibility of a Grand Retablo came under serious reconsideration. Arthur and Gaye Birtcher, long time members and supporters of the Mission Parish, formed a committee to brainstorm the project: What should it look like? What should be contained in it? How could it express the life of the Church? He invited experts in liturgical art from Spain to listen to the ideas and propose a proper design and a realistic cost estimate. They studied the Serra Chapel retablo as well as baroque retablos in Madrid, Burgos, Seville, and Salamanca. They also incorporated features especially relevant to the Mission in order to produce a unique design.

Monsignor Paul Martin, pastor of the Mission, was about to retire and thought it wise to leave such an ambitious project to his successor. However, he hoped that the retablo might contain statues honoring Saint Joseph, Saint Francis of Assisi, Blessed Junipero Serra, and Blessed Kateri Tekakwitha. His wishes were taken to heart and were honored.

The new pastor, Father Arthur A. Holquin, enthusiastically backed the project and worked with Mr. and Mrs. Birtcher to bring it about. They carefully considered various options and possibilities. Finally, their interest and perseverance transformed the ambitious dream to a beautiful and welcome reality.

My house shall be called a house of prayer,
says the Lord:
in it all who ask shall receive,
all who seek shall find, and all who knock shall
have the door opened to them.
(Mt. 21:13; Lk.11:10)

## INTERPRETATION

### *THE HOUSE OF GOD*

*Let us go rejoicing to the House of the Lord.*
*(Psalm 121:1)*

In a sense, every house of worship may be thought of as a "House of God" – a place where God dwells. As children of God, we should feel at home there. It is where we are given new life, raised in faith, nourished by word and sacrament. It is where we find sanctuary from earthly noise and annoyance. It is where, together as family, we gratefully call God, "Our Father".

### *OUR HEAVENLY HOME*

Our Father calls his children to lives of charity, service, and loving sacrifice. And when lives lived in this Spirit have run their course in this imperfect world, He welcomes them into the perfection of His Heavenly Home.

The Grand Retablo takes the literal appearance of a "House of God" and a "Heavenly Home". It has a foundation, several floors, columns, portals into the spiritual, and an adorning roof with openings to the infinite. It is an artistic imagining of God's golden home: shining, colorful, inviting, and beautiful – the Heavenly dwelling to which we are called.

*Lead us safely home to heaven,*
*to be happy with you forever.*
*(Opening Prayer,*
*Funeral Mass)*

## ✎ ELEMENTS

### *THE TRINITY*

The principal focus in God's House, of course, is God. The retablo features God as Trinity, One God in three Persons: Father, Son, and Holy Spirit. The Holy Spirit of God is seen as a pure white dove near the top of the structure. It is a traditional representation recalling the biblical appearance of the Spirit of God in the form of a dove at Christ's baptism. This dove is set on a background of golden rays shining in all directions. This represents the Spirit of God radiating gifts of inspiration, enlightenment, and sanctification.

Beneath the Holy Spirit is the sculptured image of God the Father and God the Son. God the Father is seen with a triangular halo, representing the Trinity. He is depicted as both receiving the sacrifice of His Son, Jesus crucified, and giving Him to us as a precious gift for our salvation and redemption.

*God so loved the world that He gave His only begotten Son, and His Son So loved us that He gave Himself for our salvation.*
*(Collectio Rituum, 365)*

- TRINITY -

## ADORING ANGELS

*Bless the Lord, all you angels of the Lord. Sing His glory and praise forever.*
*(Dan. 3:58)*

High up on the retablo, cherubic angels enshrine the depiction of the Triune God. There are five altogether: two each on either side of the Trinity and one – face only – at the very top peering through a cloud of glory. A sixth angel may be found towards the bottom of the image of Our Lady of Guadalupe.

*Glory to the Father and to the Son, and to the Holy Spirit, as it was in The beginning, is now, and will be forever.*

## *SALVATION*

Jesus called people to turn from sin and return to the love of their Heavenly Father. He showed them the way by His word and example. Where humanity had been proud, He would be humble. Where humanity had been disobedient, He would obey. Where humanity had failed in love, He would be true to the end. It was a new life in the Spirit of God. It was the good news (gospel) of salvation.

## *SACRIFICE*

*There is no greater love than this: to lay down one's life for one's friends.*
*(John 15:13)*

Though innocent, Jesus took upon Himself the sins of the world. By allowing Himself to be sacrificed for those sins, He became forever our Savior and Redeemer. His resurrection proclaimed victory over sin and death and gave redeemed humanity the way to eternal life and happiness.

*Dying you destroyed our death, rising you restored our life.*
*(Eucharistic Proclamation)*

### *REDEMPTION*

It is our belief that God in His love created the universe and, in it, the human family. In an ancient time, humanity betrayed God's love in an original sin of disobedience and pride. This rejection of God's will created a spiritual break, a separation that stained humanity, forfeited grace, and opened the way for misery and death. However, God in His merciful love promised a Messiah, a Savior, to repair the breach and redeem fallen humanity. God gave His Word.

*The Word became flesh and made his dwelling among us.*
*(John 1:14)*

In the course of time, Jesus the Christ came into human history as Son of Mary and Son of God. Both human and divine, He united in His person God and man. He became God with us and for us — One able to do for the human family what it was not able to do for itself.

## THE MASS

The retablo's Trinitarian sculpture is directly related to the altar. Its depiction of the Father both giving and accepting the Perfect Sacrifice on our behalf is what happens at that altar. The grace of the Lord's Supper, Calvary, and Easter are made present again. And new life in God's Holy Spirit, nourished by a Holy Communion, allows us to share in this great sacrifice of praise – and its blessing. At the altar we comply with Jesus mandate, "Do this in memory of me"(1 Cor.11: 24). At the altar we offer ourselves with Jesus as He offers Himself to Our Father. At the altar we pray our thanksgiving (Eucharist) for God's gift of "amazing grace."

*Through Him, with Him, in Him, in the unity of the Holy Spirit, All honor and glory are yours, Almighty Father, forever and ever.*
*(Eucharistic Prayer: Doxology)*

### *OUR LADY OF GUADALUPE*

Mary, the Mother of Jesus, appears on the retablo in the image and title of Our Lady of Guadalupe, Patroness of the Americas. She is also patroness of the Diocese of Orange in California. Devotion to her was familiar to the padres, soldiers, and settlers who first came to California. An image of her was brought up from New Spain (Mexico) and became part of the first religious decorations at the San Juan Capistrano Mission. This original painting still graces the Serra Chapel.

On December 9, 1531, Mary appeared to Juan Diego, a pious Indian, at Tepeyac Hill near Mexico City. She instructed him to tell Bishop Juan de Zumarraga, first Bishop of Mexico, to build a church there. In a second appearance, three days later, she told him to pick flowers and take them to the bishop. When he gathered them up in his cloak and presented them, roses fell before the bishop and the magnificent image of Mary (Our Lady of Guadalupe) appeared miraculously on his cloak. A church was built there and that image has been venerated ever since. Records of the original event and subsequent miracles attributed to Mary in this image appear very early in Mexican History.

The first sanctuary was built in 1533. In 1556, Archbishop Alonso de Montifer, second Bishop of Mexico, began the second church. In 1695, construction began on the first basilica at the foot of Tepeyac Hill. It was solemnly dedicated in 1709 (sixty years before the first California Mission at San Diego). Many additions to it followed over the years. In the 1970's, the basilica was declared dangerous because of damage caused by its gradual sinking into the soft subsoil. A new and modern basilica opened in 1976.

Over the years, Our Lady of Guadalupe has acquired many impressive titles. In 1737, she became the Patroness of Mexico City. In 1746, she became the Patroness of New Spain (Mexico, California, Guatemala, and El Salvador). In 1754, Pope Benedict XIV approved a Mass and Office to be prayed in her honor. In 1895, with papal authority, a solemn coronation of the image took place at which many of the bishops of the Americas were in attendance. In 1910, Pope Saint Pius X proclaimed her the "Virgin Patroness of Latin America." In 1935, Pope Pius XI declared her

Patroness of the Philippines. And in 1945, Pope Pius XII named her "The Queen of Mexico and Empress of the Americas." The Congregation for Divine Worship, on March 29, 1999, raised the Mass for Mary under this title to the rank of a Feast for all the countries of the Americas. This feast is celebrated on December 12th, the anniversary of Mary's last apparition to Juan Diego at Teyeyac, Mexico. On July 31, 2002, Pope John Paul II presided at ceremonies canonizing Juan Diego as a saint.

The appearance of Our Lady of Guadalupe to Saint Juan Diego is credited with drawing a large number of Indians to the Christian Faith. She is seen as reconciling the combating cultures of the European and Native Americans. She calls all to recognize their common blessing and dignity as children of God.

The image of Mary on Saint Juan Diego's cloak is a cultural mix. Her dress is European while the decorations on it are indigenous. She is pregnant and the Nahuatl symbol for the center of the universe appears over her womb, which carries Jesus the Savior.

In 1981, Bishop William Johnson, first Bishop of Orange, traveled to Mexico with Cardinal Timothy Manning and other California bishops. In the new basilica, they concelebrated Mass in honor of the 450th anniversary of the apparition of Our Lady of Guadalupe.

### *SAINT JOSEPH*

In the niche on the lower left of the retablo is the statue of Saint Joseph. As husband of Mary and guardian of Jesus, he was selected to be the patron and guardian of the whole California Mission endeavor. The Spanish missionaries and explorers prayed for his intercession to help them overcome their many difficulties and bring success to their work. In 1769, their very first year in Upper California, they were nearly forced to abandon the entire project because of serious illness and lack of supplies. Father Serra persuaded them to delay their departure until the Feast of Saint Joseph. On that day, their rescue ship was sighted and the project was saved. Down through the many years since its founding, San Juan Capistrano has celebrated March 19th, Saint Joseph's Day, as a great Mission Fiesta. It is on this day that early residents noticed the phenomenon of the return of swallows to Capistrano. Saint Joseph is honored here on the retablo for his continuing role as an important patron for the Church in California.

### *SAINT FRANCIS OF ASSISI*
### *(1182 – 1226)*

On the lower right of the retablo is the statue of Saint Francis of Assisi. His simplicity, humility, and piety attracted many others to devote themselves to Christ and lives of service. His followers became known as Franciscans and from this religious order came Father Junipero Serra and the missionaries who brought Christianity to California.

In 1776, the same year Capistrano was founded, San Francisco, "City by the Bay" and its mission were placed under the patronage of their holy founder, "San Francisco de Asis." He is recognized in this altarpiece as the spiritual father of those who began the Christian mission at San Juan Capistrano. His holy life remains a model of piety to inspire those who serve here. Just two years after Francis's death in 1226, Pope Gregory IX proclaimed his sanctity to the Universal Church in ceremonies of canonization. His feast is observed on October 4th.

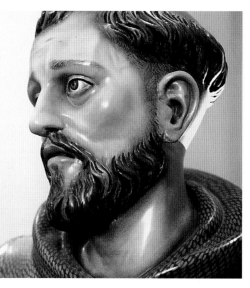

## *BLESSED JUNIPERO SERRA*
### *(1713 – 1784)*

In the niche on the upper left side of the retablo is the statue of Blessed Junipero Serra, "Apostle of the Californias." This Spanish Franciscan was a well-respected University Professor who chose to leave the comforts of home to assume the humble life of a Christian missionary. He accepted the hardships and dangers of life on the Spanish frontier because of his zeal for souls and the spread of the gospel.

In 1769, Father Serra came to Alta California where he spent the rest of his life as President of the Franciscan missionary endeavor. He was responsible for the first nine of California's twenty-one missions. He loved the Indians, whom he regarded as children of God. In 1987, Pope John Paul II beatified him in ceremonies at the Vatican. Blessed Junipero Serra is honored here both for his holiness and in proud recognition that he is the father and founder of this Mission, established on All Saints Day, November 1, 1776. His feast day is July 1st.

### *BLESSED KATERI TEKAKWITHA*
### *(c.1656 – 1680)*

In the niche on the upper right is the statue of Blessed Kateri Tekakwitha, "Lily of the Mohawks." She is the first North American Indian officially recognized by the Universal Church as "Blessed"– a model of Christian virtue. She is known to have suffered much in her young life – orphaned and somewhat disfigured in a smallpox epidemic. As a young maiden she was attracted to the Christian life and accepted baptism on Easter Sunday in 1676. This conversion and her refusal to marry made her an outcast among many of her own people. She took refuge in a Christian village at Saint Francis Xavier Mission near Montreal. There she received her First Communion and made a private vow of chastity. She soon became known for her austerity, deep personal prayer, and her great charity towards the sick and elderly. She passed away in 1680 at the age of twenty-four. Her beautiful life helped win many converts to the Christian faith. She is honored here for her inspirational life as a Christian Native American. Pope John Paul II beatified her in 1980 and her feast day is celebrated on July 14th.

Mineral

Vegetative

Animal

Human

Angelic

## *LORD OF CREATION*

*Blessed are you, Lord, God of all creation.*
*(Liturgy of the Eucharist)*

God is the beginning and end of all that is. A special feature of the basilica retablo is the symbolic representation of all the levels of God's creation. Angelic creation is represented by the figures of angels praising God. Humanity is represented by the statues of the Blessed, the Saints, and most nobly by Jesus uniting human nature with the divine. Animal life is represented by the figures of the swallows that fly about the columns. Vegetative life is seen in the carved leaves, flowers, and the grapes with their vines clinging to the retablo pillars. Mineral existence is represented by the gold leaf, which decorates the whole retablo.

## THE ALTAR

*I will go to the altar of God,*
*who gives joy to my youth. (Ps. 42)*

An altar is a raised structure or table on which sacrifices are offered for religious purposes. In Christianity, the altar is the place where Jesus is the "Priest, the altar, and the Lamb of sacrifice (Easter Preface V). It is at this table of the Lord's Supper that Jesus offers Himself to our Heavenly Father as a sacrifice for us. It is also the table of the Lord's Supper where Jesus transforms bread and wine into His very presence for us as a Blessed Sacrament. And it is from this table that Jesus invites us into a Holy Communion with Him and one another. Sharing His sacrifice and nourished by His gift of self, we are enabled to worship – to offer praise and thanksgiving.

Carved Altar

Finished Altar

Cercelee Cross

Back of Altar

Mensa with five Wound Crosses

Reliquary

Wound Cross

Reliquary Open

Because of its dignity and purpose, the altar is anointed at its dedication. It is reverenced with a bow and by the priest's kiss at the beginning and end of Mass, and by incense in solemn liturgy. And because the altar symbolizes Christ Himself, it is the center and focal point of every Christian church.

The Mission Basilica's altar is an artful composition of marble, alabaster, metal, gilding, paint, carved wood, and fine carpentry. The mensa, or top of the altar is 38.5 inches from the predella, or floor. It is a three-inch thick and six-foot square slab of green, macael marble from Alicante in Spain. Incised into the top of it are five Greek crosses. Each is gold and five inches in length. There is one cross at each corner and one at the center. They represent the five wounds of Christ: the nail wounds on his hands and feet and the spear wound on His side.

A nearly square, central pedestal supports the base of the altar. On the three sides facing the nave and the transepts, there is a cercelee cross superimposed on a quatrefoil cross. The cercelee is an ancient form of the cross with open ends that some see as the horns of a sacrificial ram. This cross is said to symbolize maturity of faith and has been commonly used in heraldry on various coats of arms. The quatrefoil consists of four, equal semicircles forming a cross.

The side of the pedestal that faces the priest celebrant is made of alabaster and ornamented with metal artwork. It is here where the relics are placed within the altar. This tradition dates back to early Christian history when churches were sometimes placed over the remains of the saints. Saint Peter's Basilica, built over his tomb, is a prime example. The Mission Basilica's altar contains the relics of a variety of saints. This is reminiscent of the Mission's founding on All Saints Day (November 1, 1776).

Also supporting the marble mensa are eight Solomonic, spiraled columns with Corinthian capitals. There are two as each corner. They are carved from cedar, then gilt and colored. Appropriately, each column is decorated with grapes, a Eucharistic symbol recalling the wine which Jesus consecrated as His own blood, shed for all and shared in Holy Communion.

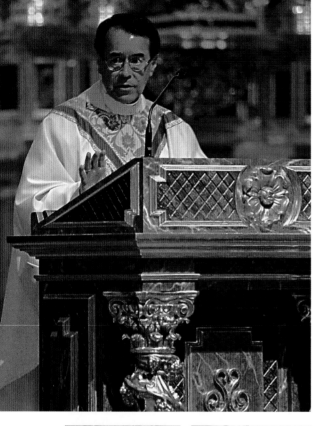

### *AMBO*

*God's word is living and effective. (Heb.4: 12)*

The word "ambo" comes from the Greek indicating an elevation. In the Greek Byzantine Rite it refers to the pulpit. It is the place in the sanctuary where the word of God is proclaimed in the Sacred Scriptures. It is the natural focal point of the Liturgy of the Word that teaches, enlightens, inspires, and nourishes the soul. It is at the ambo that the homilist preaches a reflection on that Word to the assembly. The ambo's place near the altar appropriately indicates its special relationship to the Liturgy of the Eucharist. Its construction and appearance, following the baroque style of the altar and retablo, also highlights this relationship.

*My word shall not return to me void but shall do my will, achieving the end for which I sent it.*
*(Is. 55: 11)*

## *TABERNACLE*

The word "tabernacle" comes from the Latin word for tent, tabernaculum. The concept of tent refers to the Old Testament tent of the Ark of the Covenant where God was present among his people.

The tabernacle is the sacred container where the Blessed Sacrament, consecrated at Mass, is reserved for the purpose of Holy Communion to be taken to the sick and the homebound. Because of the divine presence in the Eucharist, it also serves as a focal point for devotion and adoration. In keeping with the altar and its retablo, it is designed in a similar style. The area where the tabernacle is located is called the Blessed Sacrament Chapel.

## *STATIONS OF THE CROSS*

The Stations of the Cross are a devotional exercise in which participants prayerfully meditate on fourteen scenes of the suffering and death of Christ. The Franciscans, who took custody of the Christian shrines in the Holy Land in 1342, promoted this religious practice. Although there were a variety of ways of performing this spiritual exercise, the common practice of fourteen specific events in Christ's passion and death stems from the 18th century, the same period when the Franciscans established the California Missions. Modern practice calls for a 15th station meditating on the Resurrection.

## PHYSICAL DESCRIPTION

### *GENERAL*

In general, the Grand Retablo consists of a foundation; two levels, or floors; three lateral sections, or shrines, on each level; three pediments, or roof-like structures; and an attic. Thirty feet wide and forty-two feet high, it is constructed of cedar and is entirely covered with 24-karat gold leaf. And, in keeping with the baroque style, the whole composition is entirely ornamented.

### *A CLOSER LOOK*

For those who prefer a more detailed description, we start from the bottom up. The base, or foundation, is called the predella.

(This should not be confused with the predella in the strict liturgical sense, which actually refers to the floor on which the altar stands.) It is thirty feet long and five and a half feet high. It is made up of seven sections known as pedestals, which alternate in a projected and recessed sequence. Each is decorated with moldings encasing alternating green and red faux marble. The central section – in red – is wider and bears a carved rosette in high relief.

Above this is the banco, the immediate support of the first level. This feature is repeated as the base of the second level with its three shrines.

The central section of the first level bears the image (oil on wood) of Our Lady of Guadalupe. The image is enshrined by an hornacina (vaulted arch) composed of curved entablature containing hojarasca (a decoration of carved leaves) and a cartela (a carved, ornamental frame) containing a stylized letter "M", for Mary. Two spiraled and decorated Solomonic columns with Corinthian capitals support the arch. At the base of the Guadalupe shrine is a richly carved and colorful foliage relief.

Except for the statues themselves, the first floor shrines of Saint Joseph, on the left, and Saint Francis, on the right, have the same features. Each statue rests on a pedestal supported by a carved and colorful mensula (support bracket) decorated as foliage. The niche for the statue is framed by a double arched molding surmounted by a floral relief. The flat panel behind the statue is decorated with engraved ornamentation in silver and gold tones. To the right and to the left of each statue is a pair of Solomonic columns with Corinthian capitals. These rest on pairs of gold pedestals with faux, green marble framed by moldings. The columns rise up and support an alternation of projected and recessed entablature, decorated at the top with a running sequence of faux, green marble, complimenting the pedestal arrangement below. Each spiraled Solomonic column is beautifully decorated in relief with twisting grape vines and San Juan Capistrano's legendary swallows. These features are the same for each of the four shrines: Saint Joseph and Saint Francis of Assisi on the first level, and Blessed Junipero Serra and Blessed Kateri Tekakwitha on the second level. The only difference is that the second level shrines are surmounted by broken (opened) pediments (roof-like) structures.

Of course, the heavenly shrine of the Holy Trinity rises above all. At the shrine's bottom is a wide, narrow gold pedestal with carved foliage encased in moldings. On either side are scrolled corbels supporting highly ornamented pilasters called estribos. These support the double, semicircular arch that contains the four adoring angels. At the summit of this arch is the Holy Spirit, represented by a white dove on carved, golden rays of light. Continuing this shrine to the very top, two decorative pilasters, called estipites, support a singular structure composed of a broken pediment and a broken architrave. Surmounting it all is the copete, a large, cloud-like feature from which appears the face of an angel. The background

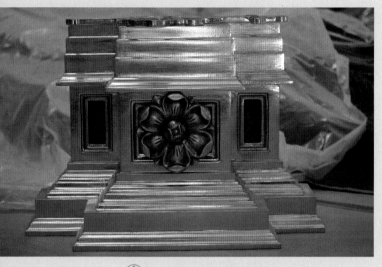

✦ Pedestal

✦ Mensula

area of the figures of God the Father and His crucified Son consists of a panel with gold and polychromatic accents. On either side of the foot of the cross are decorative features with engraved geometric pattern, moldings, and painted ornamentation. In the attic, outside the Trinity shrine, to its left and right, are similar features continuing the busy baroque style of lavish décor.

✦ Predella Base

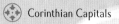

Corinthian Capitals

Column Bases

Decorative Motif

Salomonic Column

Estribos

Estipite

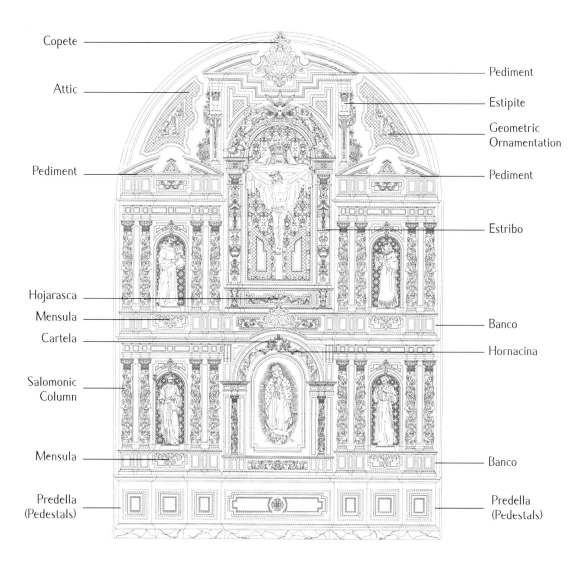

Copete

Attic

Pediment

Hojarasca

Mensula

Cartela

Salomonic
Column

Mensula

Predella
(Pedestals)

Pediment

Estipite

Geometric
Ornamentation

Pediment

Estribo

Banco

Hornacina

Banco

Predella
(Pedestals)

# CONCEPT TO
## ℘ *Reality* PRODUCTION

ℐ ILLIG

It was readily determined that the existing sanctuary floor would be unable to support the 16 ton weight of the planned retablo. The same was true of the basilica's back wall. The Illig Construction Company based in Los Angeles was chosen to remedy the problem.

Illig has been in business since 1919. Rita Illig Liebelt, president of the company, is its third generation leader. As a general contractor, the company is highly respected and has been involved for many years in major building and renovation projects, including a wide variety of important historic sites.

George Smith served as Illig's project manager for the Mission Basilica's retablo support system. Frank Johnson served as its on-site superintendent. Armando Ruiz, A.I.A. served as foundation architect and Marcelo Cairo, vice-president of John A. Martin and Associates, Inc. provided the structural engineering.

Work began on the foundation on September 25, 2006. A large section of the sanctuary floor had to be removed in order to create the retablo foundation. Because all the equipment had to come through the basilica's double doors, a special rig had to be used to drill through the soil to provide for supports. Four caissons, fifteen feet deep and 36 inches wide filled with reinforced concrete provided the principal base. A horizontal foundation of reinforced concrete, six feet wide, four feet deep, and thirty feet long, tied it all together. Above that, a 16 ton steel superstructure, 44 feet high provided the framework to which the retablo would be attached. This was an unusual fabrication because it had to

be put together without welding inside the basilica.

Following this work, the sanctuary floor was refinished and restored to match. The foundation project was concluded on January 17, 2007.

Later, when the retablo arrived from Spain, Illig provided the equipment and scaffolding needed for the Spanish workmen to assemble it. Illig's work finished when the retablo was completed and the scaffolding removed.

## ✍ TALLERES DE ARTE GRANDA (TAG)

The Spanish firm of Talleres de Arte Granda has been in the business of liturgical art for well over a hundred years. From its beginning, it has been dedicated to "speak and teach about Christ" through sacred art produced by highly skilled artists and craftsmen using the finest quality materials. Over the years, their proven work and reputation have earned them clients from all over the world.

Today, "Granda" has offices in Spain and the United States. Its headquarters, just outside Madrid, houses both offices and a factory where both Old World craftsmanship and the most modern technology blend to produce fine sacred art. It has a staff of over a hundred artists and business professionals. Its design department includes architects, interior designers, engineers, and graphic designers. Among its artists, there are painters, gilders, carpenters, sculptors, silversmiths, enamellists, and restoration specialists.

✤ Carving Blessed Serra

 Second Level

 First Level

Talleres de Arte Granda has long collected a treasure house of literature on sacred art, architecture, and techniques. It teaches and trains new artists and craftsmen in old methods and new. It is knowledgeable and capable of producing liturgical art in both classic-traditional and modern styles. Its wide-ranging capabilities allow it to manufacture every object of sacred art from the building itself to all its sacred furnishings, décor, paintings, vessels, vestments, and linens.

After various considerations, the Mission Basilica chose Talleres de Arte Granda to design and fabricate its Grand Retablo. This decision was based on Granda's capability of carrying out such detailed work in a quality manner. Arrangements were made through Mr. Manuel Suarez, Granda's Director of Project Development for the U.S.A. The design and manufacture was placed under the leadership of Mr. Juan Antonio Medina.

## CONSTRUCTION

The contract for the Grand Retablo was signed in December of 2005. A confident Talleres de Arte Granda had already begun their design work in November. Early in 2006, actual construction began at their factory just outside Madrid. It required the rest of the year to complete the massive and highly detailed altarpiece.

Under the competent direction of Juan Antonio Medina, the retablo's Design Manager, some eighty-five artisans contributed their own particular expertise to the project. Following exact specifications, they each applied their craft and transformed the conceptual design into a real, material work of art.

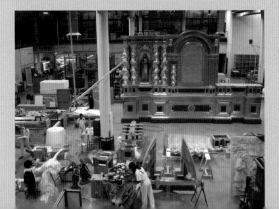

## PROCESSES

### GILDING (GOLD LEAFING)

The Grand Retablo is made of Brazilian cedar wood. It is entirely covered with 24-karat gold leaf. After the wood has been thoroughly cleaned, a layer of hot, elastic glue made from rabbit skins is applied to the wood so that it penetrates the pores of the wood. Afterwards, seven coats of thin plaster (matte gesso) are brushed or sprayed onto the surface. This gesso absorbs water allowing the gold to adhere properly. Once the gesso is dry, it is sanded until it is completely smooth. Next, layers of bole (a mixture of clay and glue made from fish skins) are added. This provides the proper surface for the adhesion of the gold leaf. Then, in a clean environment, the actual application of the gold begins.

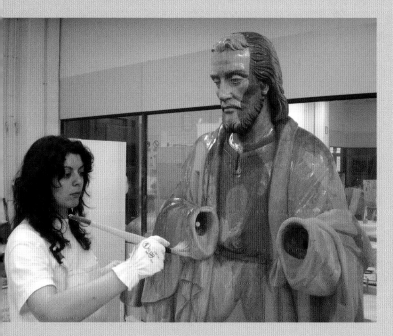

## - GILDING -

The artist (gilder) deposits small, super thin sheets of 24-karat gold leaf onto a gilder's pad. The gold is not touched by hand, since this would cause it to deteriorate. If necessary, the gold sheets are cut with a gilder's knife. They are picked up with a gilder's brush and applied to the surface. Then the gold leaf is burnished and polished with a pencil-like instrument with a smooth, curved agate tip. This produces a golden surface with a smooth and brilliant shine.

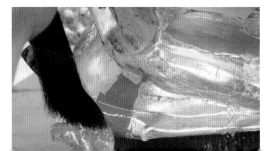

- POLYCHROME: PAINTING OVER GOLD LEAF -

## *ESTOFADO*

Wooden statues and other special items, such as columns, are machine carved to a predetermined general shape. After this, a sculptor hand-carves them to achieve a desired look. Then the items are gold leafed and polychromed (painted with various, appropriate colors). Following this, a small, scalpel-like tool is used to remove some of the paint and reveal the gold beneath. This painstaking process requires a highly skilled artist with an experienced, steady, and gentle touch. The estofado process makes possible the intricate gold designs and patterns seen, for example, on the clothing worn by those depicted in the statues. The delicate artistry involved has a pleasing overall affect, but is especially appreciated by a close-up examination. A great example of this craft is the chiseled, estofado work on the figure of Saint Joseph.

- ESTOFADO PROCESS -

## BLESSED KATERI TEKAKWITHA

- CARVED WOOD - GILDING - POLYCHROME -

# BLESSED KATERI TEKAKWITHA

- ESTOFADO -

- BLESSED KATERI TEKAKWITHA -

## ASSEMBLY

By the end of the 2006, Granda had virtually fabricated all the retablo's parts. Nevertheless, no one there could see the completed product until it was assembled in the Basilica of San Juan Capistrano. Packing and shipping itself became an art form. Every item had to be carefully placed in specifically designed packing crates and loaded into cargo containers according to a set plan. Trucks brought these to the Port of Valencia where they were shipped across the Atlantic, through the Panama Canal, and on to their destination of the Pacific coast. After their 8,000-mile journey, the containers were off-loaded at the Port of San Pedro and trucked to San Juan Capistrano.

Unpacking

Opened Crate

Transporting Statue

Assembling First Level

Although the original goal was to have the Grand Retablo in place by May of 2007, Granda's work exceeded expectations and the new, hoped for goal became March 19th, the Feast of Saint Joseph, Capistrano's Annual Swallows Day Fiesta. When the trucks carrying the retablo arrived from the Port of San Pedro on February 19, 2007, Juan Antonio Medina and his team from Spain were there to meet them and undertake the careful process of assembly. The off-loading went well and the unpacking of the crates revealed that all had arrived in good order and good condition.

First, the base of the altarpiece had to be fixed to the prepared foundation. Then each item had to be attached to the steel structure. For the next several weeks, the delicate work of assembly progressed from floor to ceiling. To everyone's delight, the work completed in good time and all was in place for the March 19th celebration. San Juan Capistrano Mission Basilica had its Grand Retablo.

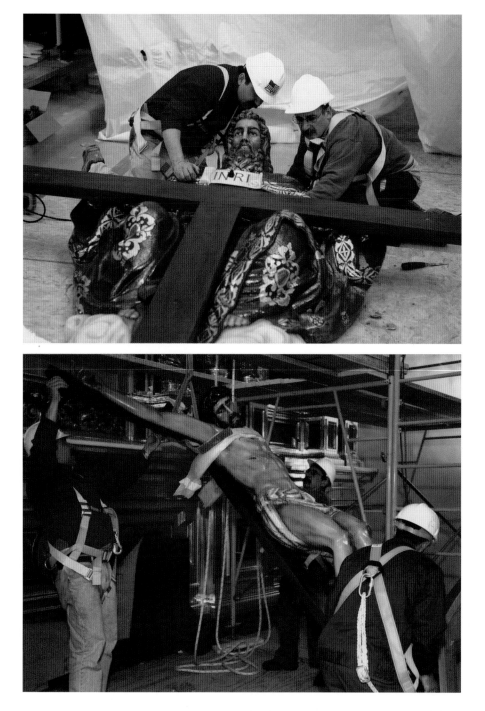

 Talleres de Arte Granda Team

# ✤ Saint Joseph Day

*March 19, 2007*

✤ BLESSING

A special Mass is celebrated in the Mission Basilica in thanksgiving for the Grand Retablo and in recognition of those who made it possible.

## ℘ BENEFACTORS

**With our love of God, and in humble gratitude for His abundant blessings, we gift this retablo to the parishioners, and pilgrims of the Mission Basilica San Juan Capistrano.**

**Arthur and Gaye Birtcher**
**Velma F. O´Brien**                    **Summer, 2007**

"The word "liturgy" means the work of the people of God. Our Basilica enhancements have indeed been the work of many gifted, talented, and generous people of God. For their support of these accomplishments, we are truly grateful.

Our beautiful altar, tabernacle, and Stations of the Cross are gifts from the Thomas J. and Erma Jean Tracy Foundation. These wonderful items are in loving memory of our friend, Thomas J. Tracy who recently passed away.

When the church was completed twenty years ago, it was the vision and passion of a number of individuals in this community that one day the interior would be completed with a magnificent Retablo that would tie this Basilica Church to its historic roots in the venerable Serra Chapel and the Great Stone Church. The passion and determination that has brought this about, has been a powerful force in the heart of Art and Gaye Birtcher, whose drive, commitment, and personal generosity has brought us to this moment. Thank you Art and Gaye. Together with the most generous bequest of Art and Gaye's dear friend, Velma O'Brien, our Retablo has been completely gifted to our Church to be a continuing source of inspiration for all who pilgrim to this historic and National Shrine."

*Very Reverend Arthur Holquin,*
*Rector/Pastor*
*Feast of Saint Joseph,*
*March 19, 2007*

# TIME *Line*

• 1776, November 1
Blessed Fray Junipero Serra founds Mission San Juan Capistrano.

• 1797, February 2
Construction begins on a Great Stone Church for Capistrano.

• 1806, September 7
Fray Estevan Tapis, President of the Missions, and California Governor Jose Joaquin de Arrillaga lead ceremonies celebrating the opening of the Great Stone Church.

• 1812, December 8
A major earthquake destroys the Great Stone Church.

• 1924, April
Monsignor St. John O'Sullivan restores the Serra Chapel and installs in it a baroque Spanish retablo, (gold altarpiece), several centuries old.

• 1982, January 31
Bishop William Johnson, first Bishop of Orange, breaks ground for a new church for Mission San Juan Capistrano.

• 1985, March 24
Bishop William Johnson presides over the blessing of eight bells donated for the new church by the Birtcher family.

• 1986, October 23
On the Feast of St. John of Capistran, Monsignor Paul Martin, Pastor, "officially" begins services in the new church.

• 1987, February 8
Cardinal Timothy Manning dedicates the church of San Juan Capistrano.

• 2000, February 14
Pope John Paul II honors the church of San Juan Capistrano with the title of Minor Basilica.

**• 2000 – 2004**
Parishioners, Arthur and Gaye Birtcher, facilitate discussions, professional consultation, and preliminary design proposals for a Grand Retablo.

**• 2003, March 19**
The U.S. National Conference of Bishops designates Mission Basilica San Juan Capistrano a National shrine.

**• 2005, November**
Talleres de Arte Granda, a liturgical arts company, begins work on the Grand Retablo.

**• 2005, December**
The contract for the Grand Retablo is signed and work is officially underway.

**• 2006**
The artists and craftsmen of Talleres de Arte Granda fabricate the Grand Retablo at their facilities near Madrid.

**• 2007, February 19**
The Grand Retablo arrives at San Juan Capistrano and assembly begins.

**• 2007, March 19**
Very Rev. Arthur A. Holquin, Rector/ Pastor, celebrates St. Joseph Day Mass in the Mission Basilica in thanksgiving for the Grand Retablo and in recognition of those who made it possible.

**• 2007, July 21**
Cardinal William Levada, Vatican Prefect of the Congregation for the Doctrine of the Faith, presides as ceremonies of dedication for the altar and retablo at Mission Basilica San Juan Capistrano.

Published by

Éditions du Signe
B.P. 94 – 67038 Strasbourg
– Cedex 2 – France
Tel (+33) 388 789 191
Fax (+33) 388 789 199
info@editionsdusigne.fr

Publishing Director
Christian Riehl

Director of Publication
Joëlle Bernhard

Publishing Assistant
Marc de Jong

Design, Layout and
Photoengraving
Atelier du Signe – 107581

Text:
Rev. William Krekelberg

Photography
Gary M. Tinnes
Troy M. Tertany

© Éditions du Signe 2007
ISBN: 978-2-7468-1860-6